AF265243

home Remodel made Easy...

by

Evelyn Fazio

Evelyn Fazio

Evelyn Fazio

Book Design and Content by Evelyn A Fazio

Cover Design and Photography by Evelyn A Fazio

Fazio, Evelyn A. (2021). *Home Remodel Made Easy*. Paperback. Self-Publisher.

Copyright © 2013 EVELYN A FAZIO

All rights reserved. No part of this publication may be reproduced in whole or in part, or stored in a retrieval system, or transmitted in any form or by any means, graphic, electronic, mechanical, photocopying, recording, or otherwise, without written permission of the publisher.

ISBN-13: 978-0-578-92675-9 Paperback (2021)

This book is dedicated to anyone who has ever taken on
"A Home Remodeling Project"

Evelyn Fazio

AboutTheAuthor

Let's just say that I know my way around a paint brush! I have done a complete remodel inside and out of my own home, and also on a commercial rental property that I owned. This book will focus mainly on my residential property.

My home required a complete makeover, just to bring it up to "livable status." Walls, flooring, kitchen, bath, landscaping and patio all needed my attention. Not one inch of the home was left untouched by the time I was done.

Knowing it would be a lengthy process, I wanted to ensure that my time and efforts would not look outdated by the time I was finished. I made it a point to keep up with the latest in design trends over the years, and decided to share what I have found with others by writing this book.

All of the material covered in this book was either from personal experience or what I have learned from visiting Model Home Design Tours.

Introduction

Let's face it! Home remodeling can be a challenge! To some it may come as a welcome adventure just waiting for you to tap into your creative spirit! To others well, maybe it's not exactly something you look forward to doing. Everyone's situation is different. Whatever your case may be, *Home Remodel Made Easy* was written with you in mind.

Whether it be small design changes or a whole new makeover, this book is a handy reference tool that just about anyone can use. Design tips and challenges (some from my own personal experiences) as well as information gathered from Model Home Design Tours can all be found here. Find out about the latest in design trends that other remodelers just like you are using, and why keeping your home updated is an important part of the remodeling process.

I hope you enjoy reading my book as much as I have enjoyed doing my research! So go ahead, pick up that hammer, dust it off and let's get busy!

It's time to start your remodeling project!

Table of Contents

Chapter One

savvysophisticatedhomeowners

Homeowners today are savvy, sophisticated and smart. They want to be sure that the time and money spent on a remodel will be a wise investment. They know that keeping informed with the latest in design trends will ensure their homes never look outdated. This can also be especially important to those who are looking to sell their homes, and want to stay competitive in today's housing market. I have found that one of the best ways to get ideas for remodeling is to go on "Design Tours." This is my favorite way to see what the latest design trends are, in order to keep my home looking updated and current.

Modelhomedesigntours

The Home Builders Association, found in most major cities, sponsors an event every year, where they showcase new homes in the area. This event, usually held every spring and fall, is open to the general public. It is a great way to tour inside a new home before it goes on the market to be sold. Only the best builders in the areas participate, so you can be assured that the latest designs and technology will be featured in this event.

Depending on the area, the homes may range in price from over a million to under one hundred thousand dollars. All the homes, regardless of price, are open to the public and are waiting for you to take a look inside. What will I find when I go? All the newest decorating and design ideas featuring colors, flooring, lighting, kitchen appliances, countertops, cabinetry, landscaping, decks, outdoor grills and anything else that a home has. In some cases there may be an entire street of new homes to browse through, every city is different.

How do I find out about this event in my area? Do a Google search on-line and type in Home Builders Association. Then look for your town or city. In Seattle, it is called "The Street Of Dreams," in Wichita it is "The Parade Of Homes," and Dallas it is named "The Big Home Tour."

Home and Garden Shows although great to attend, can only display "samples" of cabinetry, flooring or whatever they are selling. However, it is a lot different when seeing these things in an actual house. There is nothing like walking up to the door of a brand new home, turning the doorknob and going inside! IF you ever needed motivation to redecorate or remodel this is where to find it! I usually start my tour by going to the million dollar homes first, then working my way down the list. Why would anyone want to visit a million dollar home if they had no intention of buying it? For the same reason I do, to see the latest design ideas!

I would like to share with you what I have found by going on these tours. I do this event every year, and in different parts of the country. East coast to west coast, north to south and everywhere in between, although the dollar value of the home may differ, there is some commonality to what I have found. From a designer viewpoint by visiting these homes year after year, I have gotten a "feel" of what can make one home "look" more expensive then another. I will show that by simply making a few small changes in your home, you can make a **big** difference.

Evelyn Fazio

Flooring

I have noticed, when going on these model home tours, is that wood flooring is becoming more and more common. This is particularly true in medium to upper priced homes. Lower priced homes tended to use more carpet, linoleum and ceramic tile. In the medium to upper priced homes, wood flooring was found in the kitchen, dining room and living room areas. When visiting the more expensive homes on the tour, I found wood flooring was also used in the hallways as well. Carpeting was mainly used in the bedrooms, and staircases leading down to the finished basements. Over the years I have also noticed that ceramic tile is slowly being replaced by wood flooring in the entryways of the home.

Wood flooring gives a warm inviting "look" to the home, and a feeling of *class and distinction.* There are so many different types of wood flooring products to choose from now, anywhere from laminate to the more expensive designer grades of wood. Keep in mind for a fraction of the cost of real wood, you can install laminate flooring and still achieve an "expensive" look!

Decorative Molding and Trim-work

The baseboard trim molding in all of the more expensive homes, I have found is always at least five inches tall (three inches is what is commonly used in most home construction). The taller baseboard molding is similar to what was used in historic properties over one hundred years ago. Using decorative molding and trim-work *always* makes the home appear more expensive.

*This photo was taken of a kitchen visited on the Model Homes
Tour. Note the white molding and trimwork.*

Evelyn Fazio

Accent Colors

25

Accent Paint Colors! This is one key factor that all higher priced homes have! Bold accent colors on wall surfaces are widely used. It is not uncommon to find the dining area in one color and the living room or kitchen in another! The use of different color schemes was typical in older historic homes, and is still being used today. When you separate rooms with color, it gives the home a look of class and distinction!

The photo shown here was taken in the entryway of one of the homes on the tour. Notice the dark blue accent color on the wall. Separating rooms by color gives this entryway its own identity! This is a perfect example showing how effective using accent colors can be!

Paint Colors

The choice of paint color will have a definite impact in the overall look and design of the home. There was a time, many years ago, when the color white was widely used on the interior wall surfaces. I do not see that anymore. Now the color tan is widely used. Year after year, after visiting these designer model homes, I would say that 97 percent of the time I found "tan" is the color of choice! The color tan can range from medium to very dark shades depending on the amount of accent color that is desired. In all cases, the shade of tan used is always "dark enough" to create a color contrast with the rest of the elements in the design. Molding, trim-work and interior doors were usually colored in white, and when these elements are used with darker shades of tan, it really makes for a dramatic color accent in the home.

Last year when I did the model home tour, I was focused on paint colors. As soon as I entered into the home I immediately went into the utility room. Why? Because it is where the painting contractors leave the empty gallons of paint after the model home is completed. When I found a color I liked, I took down some notes then visited my local paint store and purchased the same color they used. It is a lot easier to see if you like a particular color when it is already on a wall, instead of relying on a "little paint swatch" from your local hardware store!

Choosing the right paint finish on the interior walls is also important! I very rarely see semi-gloss paint finish on wall surfaces in the home. The flat paint finish I found, is the most common for new homes and remodels.

Speaking from personal experience, in the past when my friends and family came over to visit, they never once mentioned my walls or commented on what color they were. The walls were just "there." All that has changed. Now when people come over, the First thing they remark on IS the color on the walls and the new "look" I have created! If you don't think changing the wall color in a home makes a difference, Think Again!

Artwork

One thing all homes had in common was artwork. In every home I visited on the tour, I found that each and every one of them had some type of painting on the wall. You know you are in an "upper class" high dollar home, when you enter into the bathroom area and find a large painting on the wall! Although the bathroom itself was not that large, the painting created an atmosphere of sophistication and class.

Another home on the tour, had a design piece that immediately set the "tone" for the rest of the home. It was a very large elaborate picture frame about 30 inches x 36 inches, with a mat mounted inside. The mat inside the frame contained a piece of material, possibly linen. On top of this mat, was mounted another decorative picture frame, smaller in size, about 8 inches x 10 inches. Inside the smaller of the two frames was the painting. It was a Renaissance painting by Leonardo da Vinci. This small reproduction painting mounted inside an elaborate oversized frame made for a very striking appearance! Using oversized elaborate frames with artwork as a design element makes a visual impact and adds interest to the space.

Landscaping

Landscaping plays an important part in the overall exterior design of a home. Each model home on the tour was unique in their landscape design, however all shared the same common theme. All the landscaping elements were placed on a colorful bed of rock surrounding the perimeter of the house. In some cases mulch or bark was used. In all cases the plants and bushes were small and neatly trimmed and never overpowered the overall look of the home. Large overgrown bushes or shrubs were not to be found!

Depending on location, front lawns may also be found covered entirely in rock. This is particularly evident in areas when the climate is too harsh and makes it difficult to maintain a nice green lawn. In southwestern states such as Arizona, Texas and New Mexico, rock lawns were commonly found. Cactus and other succulents along with decorative pottery are also very common in southwestern landscapes. Ornamental pieces made of rusted metal may also adorn the lawn as well.

These decorative design elements of rusted metal are cleverly crafted in the shapes of cactus plants and other desert flora. Sculptured art can withstand the temperatures of the southwestern states, requires no maintenance, and more importantly makes a great addition to the overall landscape design of the home!

Inspiration and Motivation

On a personal note, when I first started going on these tours, there were times I would come home and feel a "little depressed" because my home did not "look" like the "million dollar" home. I don't feel that way anymore. By making the right small changes you can and *will* make a difference. You can easily move your home up to the next "level of status" by drawing your inspiration from what you find when going on these home tours. I have done it and it works! The market value of your home will increase and your home will never look outdated!

Chapter Two

Latest Trends

Home designs are constantly changing. What once was common many years ago may not be the case today. As a homeowner, being informed on what the current design trends are, is an important part of the remodeling process. Keeping your home looking updated and current is the best way to maintain a competitive edge in today's housing market. What follows are some of the new designs I have found when touring model homes over the years.

Doors

All doors in the home create an element of design, whether it be interior or exterior. It is true that by simply changing out the doors, the *overall look* of the home can change very quickly from plain ordinary to upscale. Upon entering into any given home one of the easiest and quickest ways to tell if it has been updated, is to simply look at what style doors are being used.

Interior

"Flat Panel Slab" doors also referred to as "Lauan" doors, were popular many years ago, but a lot has changed since then. The "Raised Six Panel" and newer models have since taken their place. The "Raised Six Panel" interior door style has been around now for several years, and it is *still* the most commonly seen door style found in new homes and remodels. This design has stood the test of time, and for that reason I have named this door style the "new standard." It is very versatile, and can be found in both interior and exterior locations.

Raised Six Panel

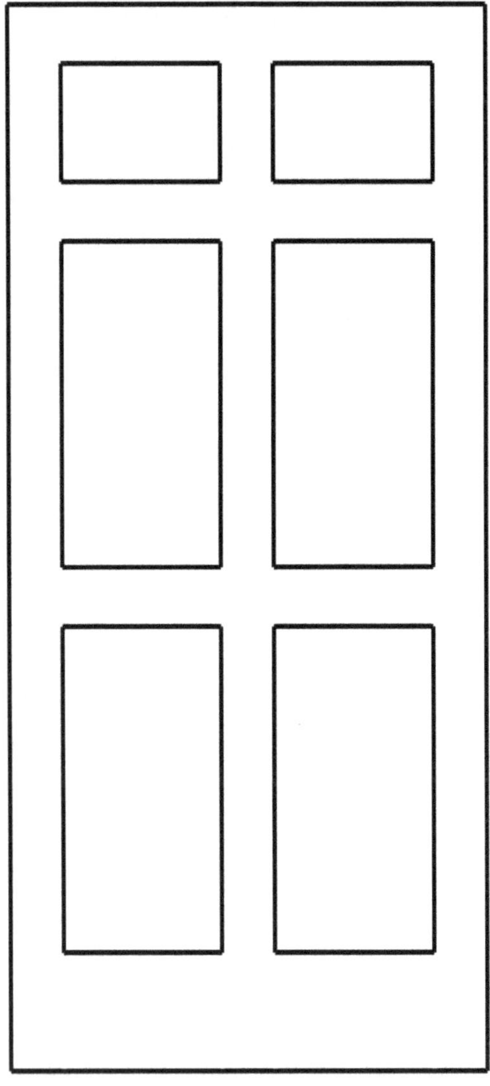

Now that we have established the "Raised Six Panel" as the "new" baseline model, what are some of the other door designs being used? The answer to that question is to simply state "History repeats itself!" Many of the new style doors are patterned after what once was popular over a hundred years ago! Old vintage door designs are becoming more and more common, especially in the moderate to upper priced homes. There are so many vintage designs being used now, that it is hard to say which one is the most popular! In any case however, it is safe to say that the old vintage designs are now becoming the new **chic!**

onepanelshaker.twopanelplank.
threepanelmission.fourpanelsquare.

Exterior Doors

Just like interior doors, the exterior door styles can also vary anywhere from the common "Raised Six Panel" to the more upscale designs. On more elaborate priced homes, exterior doors may also be made of thick solid glass with beveled edging complete with intricate artwork! Although interior and exterior doors share similar designs styles, there are some noticeable differences. One is the choice of paint color used. Interior doors are usually painted in white, however that is not the case for exterior doors. I have found that exterior doors are most often done in bold colors. Also the height of the exterior door can be eight feet or taller! This is especially common in the moderate to higher priced homes. The combination of height and bold color accents makes for a dramatic appearance in the entryway!

Hardware - Knobs, Hinges and More!

Door hardware, including knobs and hinges have taken on a class all their own. One style does not fit all anymore. Depending on the type of door style being used will also determine which hardware goes with it. And…. there are as many variations of door hardware as there are door styles! When visiting the new model homes, very rarely did I find gold colored door knobs or hinges on the interior doors. That is because that style hardware worked well at one time with the "Flat Panel" doors, and as was previously mentioned, the "Flat Panel" interior doors are not commonly used anymore in new home construction. Model home trends have shown that the "Raised Six Panel" and newer design models have pewter, black or dark colored brass hardware. Just as door styles have changed over the years so has the hardware as well. Door handles also have taken on a whole new level. Round, oblong and lever shaped design handles that were common hundreds of years ago, are now making a comeback! Old vintage doors and their hardware are now taking the lead in new home designer trends.

Although gold colored hardware may not be commonly used on interior doors anymore, for exterior doors it is a whole different story! In new home construction, as you recall, the exterior doors are commonly painted in bold vivid colors. The contrast of using gold against the bold accent color of the exterior door makes it stand out as a designer element! This is one example of how gold colored hardware can be used as an asset and contributes to the overall design of the home's entryway!

Updating a "Flat Panel" Door

We have gone over a lot of information up to this point, concerning how door designs have changed over the years. I would like to also offer a suggestion at this time on how one might update their own door design, especially if the home has "Flat Panel Slab" or "Lauan" style doors. Overall the update is really not that hard to do for most individuals, and you do not even have to take the door off the hinges! Keep in mind though, it will take a little bit of work and you do need to have some tools handy.

I have carefully selected which designs would be perfect candidates for this modification, as not all will qualify. Doors that share the same basic *flat panel profile* are the ones that will be chosen. The "Three Panel Mission," "Two Panel" and "Five Panel Equal" are all possible candidates for this modification that you can easily work with creating that new look!

Flat Panel Slab

OK, here goes! First, I want you to take another look at the "Flat Panel Slab" door again, only this time more closely. What I want to point out here is that the "Flat Panel Slab" is just that, a flat surface and nothing more. Many of the new design models also start out with the same flat surface as well. What makes the difference is what is *added* to the flat surface, thus enabling it to take on a whole new look! I discovered this while doing my research on how doors have changed over the years and what commonality they had between them. I will be using the "Three Panel Mission" style in my example.

Three Panel Mission

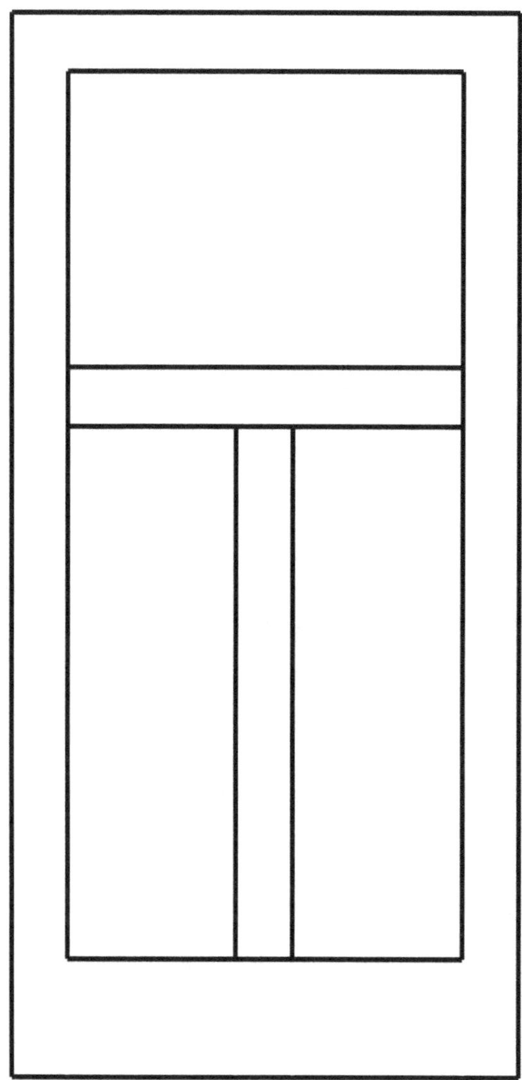

The door can remain on the hinges, however you do have to remove the door knob when doing this modification. On the "Three Panel Mission," the outer edges of the door panel have an extra piece of wood attached that goes from the top of the door to the bottom. This extra piece is *about* four and one-half inches wide and three-quarter inch thick. Attach this piece of wood around the three outer edges, the top and both sides, and for now just leave the bottom edge of the door alone.

Take the same size piece of wood and make a horizontal piece going across the door panel about two-thirds of the way up. This new horizontal piece will be cut to fit inside the new outer edges you just created. Now we will do the bottom edge of the door. The bottom edge will be using a piece of wood only this time it will be eight inches wide instead of four and one-half. This gives a distinct design element to the door. Still with us? Great! We are almost done!

Now we will create the rest of the door modification using the same size piece of wood that was used earlier, the one that is four and one-half inches wide. Using this same size piece of wood again, make a vertical piece dividing the door in half. Place it under the horizontal one, that you created earlier, so that it creates two new panels on the lower part of the door surface. What you have now created is a large letter "T". This last step creates an enclosed area that looks like two separate panels on the door.

Finally, before you replace the doorknob, a hole will have to be cut. There is a handy tool that can be purchased at your local hardware store that can help you do this. Also, the door thickness has now been increased because we have added another piece of wood on top of the door surface panel. This may require relocating the doorstop in order to have the door close properly. Do the other side of the door as well, repeating the same steps again. Once both sides have been completed, paint or stain as desired. Congratulations, you are done! Your "Flat Panel Slab" door has now been changed into a "Three Panel Mission," and you have just updated the look of your home!

Other examples to try are the "Two Panel" and the "Five Panel Equal." "The Five Panel Equal" has such a striking bold geometric design pattern, so why not choose a bold accent color as well? Be creative and have **FUN** when using color in your home!

Two Panel

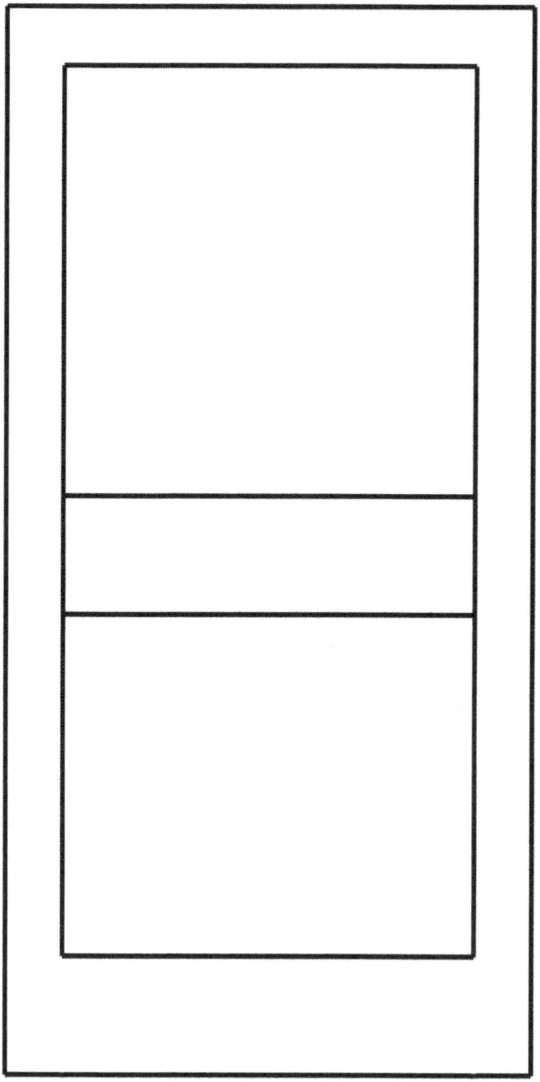

Five Panel Equal

Evelyn Fazio

Stained Concrete

56

There was a time when only the wealthy could afford to have their entryways paved in natural stone from a quarry. Stone pieces from any quarry can be costly. Natural stone entryways and patios were simply out of reach for the average homeowner. All that has changed now with the introduction of "Stained Concrete." The look of natural stone can now easily be done *and* at a very affordable price.

I first learned of the stained concrete technique, when going on these model home design tours. Upon walking up the pathway into one of the models, I remember admiring the look of natural stone beneath my feet. And indeed it did appear that way because the tonal color variations were there, along with the irregular shapes of stone and surface texture. Why was I to think anything else? Once inside the home I didn't give it another thought until I overheard one man ask the realtor "Is that stained concrete in the basement?" Her reply was "Yes."

Curious to see what he was talking about I proceeded to go downstairs. I remember patiently waiting for the crowd of onlookers to move away, so I could take a closer look at the floor. Looking more closely I realized that the concrete floor had taken on the look of natural stone! At that point I realized that the pathway I had just recently walked on, leading up to the front door, was not stone at all, but "Stained Concrete!" "What an ingenious idea!", I said to myself.

Having a curious and analytical mind I proceeded to figure out just how they did this. Upon doing some research I came up with this finding. The process is really quite simple. First the wet concrete is poured in the desired location (walkway, pathway, entryway or floor area). Then while the concrete is still wet it is "stamped" with a pre-designed template made up of irregular shapes, taking on the look of natural stone. At the proper time a stain is applied using different shades of tonal color. The different variations of color is what makes it "look" like natural stone.

One of the first few houses I looked at when I started my home tour, was the house with the stained concrete pathway and basement floor. Also take note that I visited close to over one hundred homes on this event before I was through. I can honestly say that every home I saw after that, no matter how elaborate or extravagant it may have been, if the entryway leading up to the front door was just ordinary concrete, it simply did not measure up. Every home I saw after that on this home tour, if it didn't have a stained concrete pathway leading up to the door, well quite honestly it was just "plain boring!" I *cannot* over emphasize the design impact that using "Stained Concrete" had created. The curb appeal, not to mention the increase property value because of this, is not to be overlooked. To know the cost of achieving a look of natural stone for a fraction of the cost of the real thing, is nothing short of being "Spectacular!"

Evelyn Fazio

Solar Energy Efficient Homes

As more consumers become knowledgeable about energy efficiency and its cost saving benefits, they in turn are demanding builders to provide more energy efficient homes.

Studies have shown that using **solar energy** in the home far outweighs conventional electric and heating/cooling methods. Builders have taken note of this, and now solar energy options can be found in many new homes on the market.

Just to give a quick perspective of what the cost savings are, I asked two individuals how much their monthly electric bills were once they switched to solar. One person (my uncle) lives on the West coast, and the other person lives in the Midwest. Neither of them knew each other. Two separate states two different extremes in climate temperature. However, when asked the same question how much their monthly electric bill was, BOTH of them gave the same answer. Each one said "About twenty-five dollars a month!" I don't know about you, but I would *love* to have a twenty-five dollar a month electric bill in the summer and winter seasons! Solar energy speaks for itself, and you can be assured that the next home I buy *will* have a solar panel on the roof!

Chapter Three

decoratingTips

Decorating tips are like handy tools that can help us through the remodeling process. Some tips may be the answer to finding that missing piece to the puzzle that we just couldn't seem to figure out. Others may be answers to commonly asked questions. In any case there can never be too many decorating tips to choose from.

This section of my book covers tips anywhere from working with narrow walls to building a stone patio! Also included is information on how color plays an important role in the remodeling process, and a "Do-It-Yourself" project for updating cabinetry!

Decorating a Narrow Wall

What is the best way to decorate a narrow width wall? When hanging a painting on a narrow wall, most people assume that a small size picture and frame are their only option. Absolutely Not True! Actually, it is just the opposite! Did you know that walls with narrow widths can be made to appear larger?

Allow me to explain. When people come into a home and see a narrow width wall with nothing on it, all they will focus on is the wall and how narrow it is. However, take that same wall and hang a long vertical picture frame, then the eye will focus on the size of the frame and not the wall itself. In doing so, the wall will "appear" to be wider than what it actually is.

As an example, the wall is 30 inches wide. Hang a picture frame about 24 inches wide by 28 inches tall, or 24 inches wide by 30 inches tall, with about a three inch margin from the edge of frame to the edge of the wall on both sides.

The painting and frame will now become the focal point on the wall. The viewer will now focus on the large size of the frame and not the wall itself. The result is now you have created an illusion of space!

Decorating Narrow Walls More Ideas

Most people think decorating a narrow wall is a challenge, however it may be easier than you think! Narrow walls have more possibilities than any other walls in the house. When you start hanging objects on narrow width walls, you will find the opportunities are endless!

As an example, narrow walls in bathrooms can be decorated with large seashells creating a beach theme. In the hallway, take a large straw hat and decorate the brim with flowers and a long ribbon sash hanging down for a dramatic effect. In a little girls room take a pair of ballet slippers, tie them together with a long wide ribbon hanging down. Love Music? Hang a large decorative music note on the narrow wall. The objects you hang on a narrow wall will not appear "lost" as they would on a larger wall because they will be contained in a narrow space. Using large objects will fill up the narrow space, making the wall appear wider.

When choosing objects think in terms of hobbies, room themes or special interests you have. Run out of ideas? Hobby and craft stores are a great place to go. Take another look at your narrow walls again, and you will find it is not the narrow width that is limiting you, but only your imagination.

Decorating Ideas for Small Spaces

Decorating in small spaces can be a challenge. Some rooms or areas in the home seem almost impossible to do anything with! However, I believe every space, no matter how small can have accent and create visual interest. My article will address this topic, and hopefully help to offer some solutions.

A small bathroom is a classic example of this problem. In a small bathroom there is barely enough space for the tub, toilet and sink, and not too much room to walk around! What design ideas can I possible use in this room? In a previous article, I spoke about decorating narrow walls. (refer to "Decorating A Narrow Wall" topic) I will use the same design techniques there and apply it to this small bathroom.

In this photo we see an oversized painting placed above the toilet. The oversized painting creates accent and draws interest to the space. Immediately upon entering the room, we notice this painting on the wall. It becomes the "focal point" in the room. The size of the painting helps to make the space in this small room "appear" to be larger. Notice also, this painting is not placed in a picture frame. The painting is not "confined" in an area, in this case in a frame. Because the room itself is so small, the illusion of "confinement" is purposely left out. This subtle design technique also helps to make the area in the room *appear* larger, creating an illusion of space. This small bathroom may have been overlooked before because it was a design challenge. However, by adding a few small changes, this small room can now claim its own "identity" in the home. Adding accents and interest to a small area is one way of solving the problem of decorating in small spaces.

This photo was taken of a small bathroom that I visited on the

Model Homes Tour, showing an example of a design idea used in a small space.

Decorating Small Areas Using Visual Space

You can decorate small rooms and areas in the home very easily by using "visual or open space." Placing clear, transparent or translucent objects in the room, along with "open design elements" will help to create an illusion of space, making the area "appear" larger.

Dining room table tops, or small end table tops, tall pedestals and bookcases are just some of the things that can use this design technique. Try using glass (whether clear or frosted), plexiglass material (clear or colored) or wire mesh material in your room elements. Each of these elements use "open visual space" as part of the design. The objects will not be using "solid" material, therefore not blocking the view of the room.

Try placing a vase of flowers or a piece or artwork on top of a tall glass pedestal using this technique. You will be adding interest to the room without sacrificing visual space. Open free standing bookcases can be used as room dividers, where you can place artwork or books on the shelves. Although all of these objects may be taking up "actual space" in the room, by using "open design techniques" or visual space, they will not make the room look crowded.

Using Color

Hang a New Painting!

Sometimes one of the easiest ways to redecorate a room is to just simply hang a new painting. "The right painting can change the look or mood of a room in an instant!" Whatever your decorating theme is, hanging a painting might just be the answer you are looking for!

Paintings Need Elbow Room!

The best way to show off a painting, is not to crowd the area around it. The painting will have more design impact when it is given its own space on the wall. Try not to hang the painting near other objects in the room that may distract from it.

Working with Wallpaper Background

Hanging artwork on a busy wallpaper background can be a challenge! The painting will seem to "disappear" and become "lost" on the wall. One way to avoid this is to place a three inch or wider mat border inside the frame. Be sure to choose a color that works with both the painting and the wallpaper background. In doing so, the painting will now maintain its own "identity" on the wall, while still being in harmony with the rest of the wallpaper background.

Using Accent Colors For Impact

Accent Colors added to a room can make a visual statement as well as add impact to your design space. However, choosing the right place for the accent color must be done carefully. The purpose of the accent is to draw attention to detail in the space. This detail can be artwork on a wall, or any part of the space that you want to call separate from the rest of the room.

To help with the choice of the accent color, the owner needs to ask themselves a few questions. First, what is the size of the space the accent will be used in? Second, what type of lighting will be coming into the space? Choosing a very dark accent color would prove no purpose if the light coming into the room was so dark it could not be seen. Lastly, consider the other elements in the space. How will the other colors in the room work with the accent color? The color chosen should compliment the other colors on the wall. For example, if you chose a pastel color for the accent, but the other walls had darker color tones, the two together would not work. The two colors would cancel each other out ruining the design effect in the room. Consider the area the accent color will be used on. Keep in mind also, if you are planning on placing the accent color on a large area, it should not become the dominate color in the room by overpowering the other colors.

When one enters into my home, the first thing they see is the accent wall I have created. Although I had a small space to work with, I chose a wall that was separate from the rest to place my accent color on. In doing so I achieved a separate "Block of Color" and in turn gave the illusion of making the overall space appear larger. The color I chose was a sage green and upon entering the home it immediately creates a feeling of "elegance and class" to the visitor. Using an accent color can also make the trim molding and baseboard stand out creating a design statement if so desired.

Had I chosen not to have an accent color, my walls would all be the same monotone color in the room. My goal was to create an impact by creating a contrast with color, in the small space I was given to work with. In choosing an accent color for my room in the right area, I feel that I have achieved this.

Using Color to Create Dimension

By simply choosing different shades of the same color, you can create the illusion of dimension and space. Creating the "look" of shadows on objects can help to create this illusion. I will use a bookcase as an example to demonstrate this idea. Start out with two cans of paint color. The only difference is one color will be a slightly lighter shade than the other. (It must be the same color, only one or two shades lighter) Take the darker of the two colors and paint the back wall of the bookcase. Then take the lighter of the two shades of color, and paint the shelves in the bookcase. The very "subtle" change of color from the back wall against the shelves will seem to create a "shadow look" on the shelves. By creating a "shadow look" on the shelves, you will be adding the look of dimension, and in doing so you have created the illusion of space and depth.

How to Reduce the Look of Clutter

Reducing clutter is a challenge that almost everyone faces from time to time. Obviously, the best way to reduce clutter is simply to get rid of it, and there are many articles you can read to help you achieve this. However sometimes, reducing clutter may not always be that easy for us to do.

Clutter can enter into our lives in many different ways. Perhaps we have just moved into a new home and everything is scattered all over. We find ourselves living like this for a while, until we find a place for everything to go. Or, maybe we have outgrown the home we live in now, and there is no place for all the clutter to go. And then there is the third scenario, which is the worst of all three. Someone in our home, whether it be a family member, spouse or grandparent is a "collector" of things. These knickknacks, ornaments and other memorabilia, he or she collects, over a period of time, fill up the shelves, and although they have a special significance to the collector, to everyone else it simply appears as clutter. As a result, these items remain and become a permanent distraction in the room.

This article is about how to achieve a balance, and try to reduce the "look" of clutter in the home. Can clutter and class co-exist? The answer may surprise you. To illustrate my point, I will use several examples. My first example is by taking an "imaginary visit" to an elaborate home. For the sake of simplicity, this elaborate home is without furniture. As you enter into the home, you immediately take note of all the design elements, colors and features of the home. However, in the corner of the room, on the floor, you notice a pile of magazines, books and papers. This pile of clutter does not become the focal point in the room. The design elements, colors and features become the dominating factors. The pile of clutter in the corner, is a "distraction", but it does not take away from the overall "look" of the home. In this example the "look" and appearance of clutter has been reduced.

Allow me to go a step further, and show how using accent colors can also help to reduce the look of clutter. Mrs. Jones and Mrs. Smith both have identical houses on the same street. The living room in each of their homes both have the same wall color. Both homes have built in wall units in the living room, each with the same amount of clutter on the shelves. The wall unit in Mrs. Jones's home is painted in the same color as the rest of the room. The unit "blends" into the space and almost becomes "invisible." The clutter on the shelves in her home now becomes the focal point in the room.

However, Mrs. Smith, given the same set of conditions, has chosen to use accent colors to help reduce the look of clutter. She paints her wall unit in a contrasting color and installs trim molding around it to frame out the space. The accent color she chose has just enough contrast to make a visual impact, while still working with the rest of the colors in the space. Her wall unit has now become a "design element" in the room. In her home, the wall unit becomes the focal point, not the clutter on the shelves. By using accent colors and design elements to create visual impact, Mrs. Smith has managed to reduce the appearance or "look" of clutter in her home.

Updating A "Raised Panel" Cabinet Door

The outside surface of the "Raised Panel" doors on my bathroom vanity had well, seen better days. There were water stains on the surface, and the protective finish had since worn off. At this point, most people would simply go and purchase the same style doors again and replace new. After all, the "Raised Panel" door style is very common and replacing it could easily be done.

The inside of my cabinet doors however, were in near perfect condition. Also after taking another quick look, I realized that I actually preferred the inside design better than the "Raised Panel!" It was the same door design I remember haven seen when going on the model home tours. The design consisted of a flat panel surface with the outer edges of the cabinet door covered with an extra piece of wood, about 1/4 inch thick and three inches wide. This design style of cabinetry is called the "Shaker" pattern. A simplistic design yet very classy!

Shaker Design

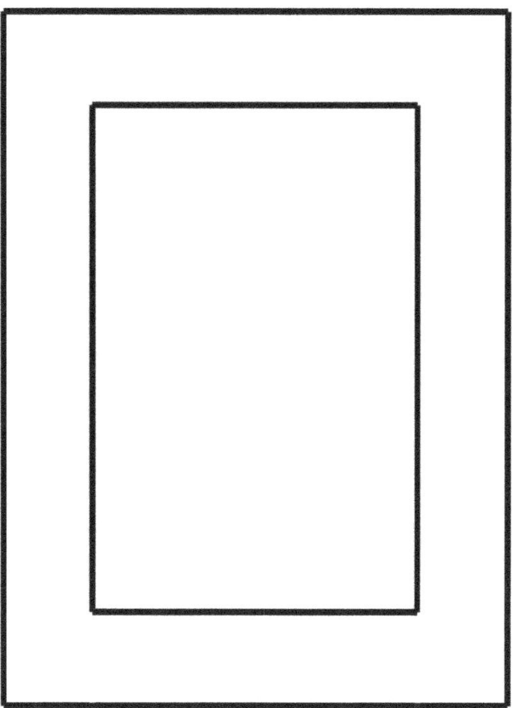

As I had been following the design trends in cabinetry over the years, I knew this was an option for me to consider. I was pleasantly surprised when I then realized, that just by reversing my cabinet doors inside out, I could instantly create a remodel update!

To complete the door remodel, I then covered the old raised panel with a piece of wood cut to size. Next I drilled new holes, covering the old with wood filler, and reversed the hinges to attach to the new outside surface. I then applied a wood stain finish to match the rest of the door completing my design update. My new "Shaker" cabinet doors look fantastic, and all I did was simply use what I had turning my doors inside out!

Stone Patio

When one thinks of installing a patio, most often the traditional cement concrete slab is the first thing that comes to mind. However did you know that instead of using the traditional cement patio, a stone patio can be used in its place? A stone patio is easy to maintain and virtually weather proof. Patios made of stone pebbles will not crack or deteriorate and will maintain their color. A wide variety of stone color choices are available to choice from, and the outside contour can easily be designed with "pound in" edge molding. Also if you wish to change the contour shape at any time, it is as simple as adjusting the edge molding and repositioning as needed with a rubber mallet.

If you happen to live in a harsh climate, a "Stone Patio" may be the better option. Cement patios overtime will tend to crack and settle into the ground surface. At that point you have two options. Either remove the entire cement slab and replace new, or try to patch up the cracks as best you can. Keep in mind the removal and reinstalling of a cement patio can be a costly job for the homeowner.

I was faced with this decision, and chose to go with the "Stone Patio" after my cement slab was removed. Choosing a stone patio was something I could do myself, and saved me a lot of money in the end. Once my cracked, and sunken cement slab had been excavated, the ground was filled in and leveled off. A weed barrier was installed on top of the dirt surface, and fasten down securely as needed. This was done in order to maintain the nice appearance of the stone patio. The contour shape of the patio was laid out to blend in with the rest of my landscaping, giving a nice neat seamless appearance. I chose a beautiful color of rainbow rock for the patio, the same color rock that I already had in my flower beds around the perimeter of my home. Once the job was completed, the new "Stone Patio" addition had become an asset to my overall landscaping design, and it is maintenance free!

Evelyn Fazio

Notes for Future Projects

Evelyn Fazio

Notes for Future Projects

Chapter Four

designChallenges

It happens to the best of us. We start our remodeling projects with all good intentions. We gather up our information, assemble all of the tools that we will be using, and feel confident that we are prepared to begin. Then it happens. Something unexpected comes up and stops us in our tracks, and suddenly we are faced with an unwelcome design challenge! Some challenges may be just a temporary set back, and we can continue on without too much problem. Others well, maybe it will take awhile to figure out *just* what to do.

Facing Challenges

In this section we will discuss some of the design challenges that homeowners may run into. Find out how lighting plays a role when planning your design, and how to choose the right paint color. Also included are tiling patterns for narrow areas, and how to plan your design layouts when faced with irregular floor plans. These are some of the same challenges I faced when doing my own remodeling, and how I overcame each and every one of them.

Accent Colors, Shadows and Light

When choosing the correct color of paint you need to keep in mind the light source falling on the surfaces to be painted. Will there be a lot of natural light coming into the space? Does the area have any shadows? Given any two wall surfaces and apply the same color to each, you will find after the color is applied it may not always "appear" exactly the same on both wall surfaces. That is because shadow and light play a major role in how colors appears on any given surface.

Before I begin this topic, allow me to give a brief intro into one of the design challenges I faced on one of my interior decorating projects. I wanted to choose an accent color and apply it to two adjacent wall surfaces in my home. To simplify, think of a cube with two adjacent sides. One side of the cube faces east and the other south. The "east" wall which is the living room/dining room area, has a lot of natural light, and the "south" wall is in the hallway with very little light and a lot of shadows. My goal was to use an accent color that would work in both places. The color needed to be dark enough to provide a good contrast in the living room/dining room area, but not too dark when used in the hallway. As any decorator would do, I tried out several paint swatches, and decided on the one I thought would be the best fit, given two sets of lighting conditions. I purchased a quart size can in my chosen color to use as my "demo" paint. I painted my own color swatch and held it up to both wall surfaces and it was a perfect fit. Next I went back to the paint store to purchase a gallon of paint in the same color, enough to cover both wall surfaces.

This is when the **"drama"** begins.

A few days later, anxious to get started on my new design project, I opened the gallon of paint I just purchased, and immediately upon opening noticed something was different. The color was 3 to 4 shades darker than the quart size I had originally bought. I checked the color name again, and the paint formula on the lid to the one on the quart size can and it was identical. Not quite knowing why it appeared different, I told myself not to worry, paint has a tendency to change color after it dries. Eager to get started, I proceeded to paint the two wall surfaces, starting with the hallway first. Then I waited for the paint to dry. Well, it dried, and it dried, and it dried and it never lightened up! What Happened ?? **%^$##@%%$$!! I quickly came to the horrible realization that I had been given two completely different colors of paint, one much darker than the other! After giving myself some time to get over the initial shock of what just happened, I began to regroup and assess my new situation. I decided I could "live" with the color on the east wall, as the living room/dining room area had an abundance of natural light coming into the space. However, in the hallway the color was way too dark. The new "honey oak" wood flooring in the hallway that I had spent so much time and effort installing, was almost "invisible" now because of the dominance of this color. And so my dilemma began.

Having only a quart size can in the "right color" to use I knew it would not be enough to paint both wall surfaces, and I did not want to spend another $20 buying another can of paint. Even if I did, whose to say the 3rd color of paint would match either of the two? I decided to take a break from this project and give myself time to figure out how I was going to approach this new "problem." After a period of time had passed, I came to a final decision. What I proceeded to do was to paint over the darker shade (what I call the "mistake" color), with the lighter shade of color I originally wanted. The lighter shade was only to be applied in the hallway, and not on the living room wall. Because of the sharp contrast between the two colors, I was careful not to let both colors appear on the same wall surface. There could be "NO" visible paint line! This can prove to be a challenge, however, I was able to do this without too much problem. When finished, there was no way anyone could tell that two different shades of color were used. In fact, both wall surfaces appeared to have the same color!

How did I pull this off? Well, remember earlier when I mentioned how light and shadow can change the way color looks on two different surfaces? In my case, I had just enough shadow and lack of light in the hallway area to "darken" the lighter shade of color, AND.... I had enough natural light in the living room/dining room area to "lighten" up the darker shade of color. As a result, even though one color was 3 - 4 shades darker than the other, when applied correctly to 2 different surfaces with 2 different lighting conditions, the both colors "appeared" to be exactly the same.

Every now and then I think back and wonder. Which was truly the "correct" shade for this color of paint? Was it the lighter shade I originally chose, or was it the "darker" shade (the "mistake" color)? Sometimes it is best to leave the mystery unsolved. All I know is, that by using two different shades of color, I managed to achieve the result I was looking for, and I could not be more pleased with the outcome! At this point, I feel it is safe to say, sometimes a "Mistake" can turn into a "Blessing."

How to Choose The Right Color of Tan Paint

Given any group of ten individuals and ask each of them to choose a color of tan, and you will get back ten different shades of color. Ask why, and the answer is simple. There is no one shade of tan. Tan can be made up of many different colors. Yellow, red, brown, green and even black undertones are all possible colors that make up the color tan. The homeowner looking to redecorate by choosing a base color for their home is faced with a myriad of shades to choose from. This task can be overwhelming to say the least. I know, because I found this to be the case when decorating my own home.

To help with the choice of which shade of tan, the owner needs to ask themselves a few questions. One, what is the size room or space the color will be going in. Second, what type of lighting will be coming into the space. Will there be much natural light? The last question to ask is "What are the other colors in the room that the tan color will be working with?" Having at least a plan for approaching the task of choosing the right shade of tan, will make the problem a little easier.

In my case I wanted the color tan I chose to be a definite contrast with the ceiling color. Using color to create contrast is an excellent way to add interest to the space. In choosing a contrast, I needed to go much darker that the white ceiling. However, the space I was working with was a small area, with not much natural light. Choosing a darker shade of tan for the sake of contrast would sacrifice making the room look smaller, closing in on the space. I did not want a shade with warm yellow or red tones, as that would not go with the rest of my color scheme.

To solve the problem I chose a tan with "Putty" based undertones. Choosing a toned down shade of tan with no yellow, green or gold undertones, turned out to be the best choice for my home. I then could easily hang my artwork and color accent pieces tying the whole look together. The process of selecting the right shade of tan can be challenging, however when done correctly, the result is worth it.

Tile Patterns for Narrow Places

Laying tile in a narrow width area can pose some problems. No matter which design pattern you choose the area is still going to remain narrow when finished. Right? Well, yes and no. Choosing the correct tiling pattern will make a difference, and although the area itself will not change, the look will *appear* wider depending on the pattern you choose.

Cobblestone Pattern

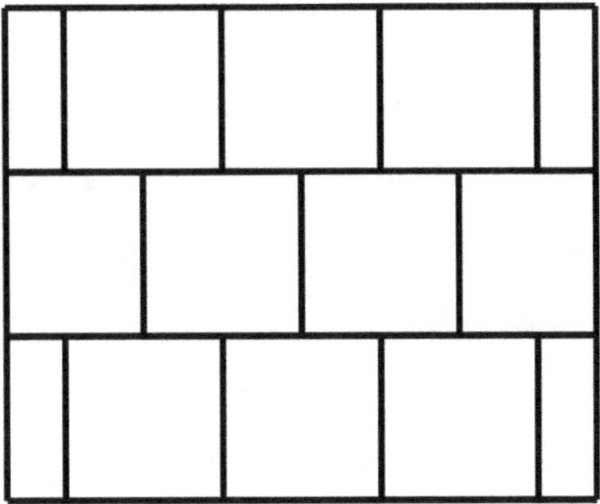

Linear Rows and Columns

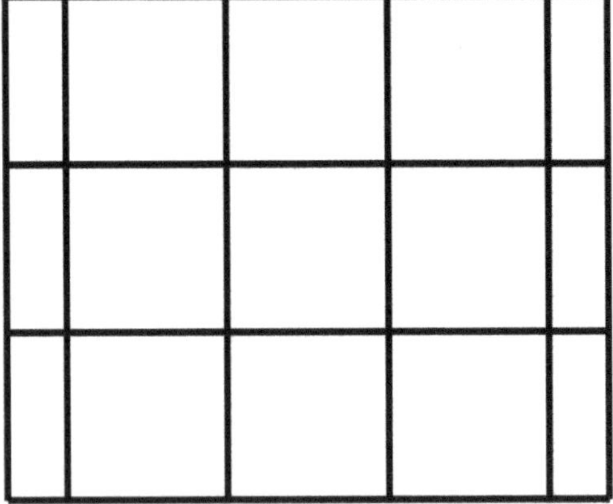

The entryway in my home was approximately forty-five inches wide. In this narrow area I decided to use a "cobblestone" pattern. The tiles in this pattern were staggered, not one lined up on top of the other in rows. In choosing this pattern, when my tiling project was completed, the narrow entryway area *appeared* to be wider. That is because the eye was now focused on the *width* of the staggered pattern, and not the narrow linear rows and columns.

Color also makes a difference when working with narrow areas. A light stone gray ceramic tile with platinum grout was what I used. By using the right combination of color, grout and tiling pattern I was able to achieve the result I was looking for.

Working With Irregular Floor Plans

Working with irregular floor patterns can be very challenging. This was one of the problems I faced when designing my flooring project. My project was to install laminate flooring in the hallway where the two wall surfaces were unequal in length. The length of one side of the hallway extended about two feet longer than the other. This presented a problem as there was no clear dividing line sectioning off the hallway from the rest of the house. My goal was to somehow "tie in" both sides making it appear as a separate hallway area. It was in this area that I wished to lay my laminate flooring.

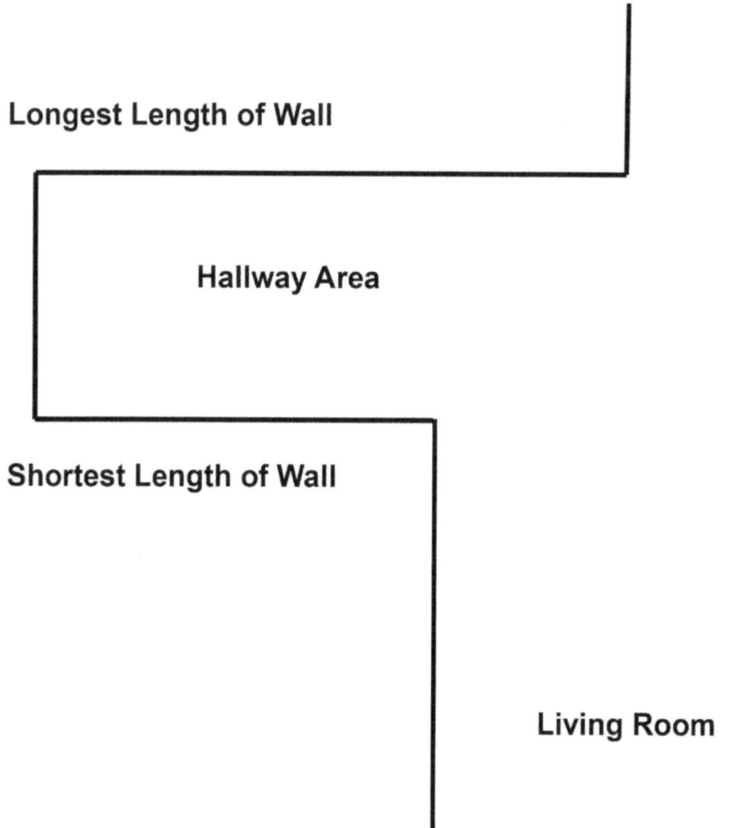

I must admit, it took awhile before I came up with a solution to this challenge. It wasn't something I could read in a book or look up in an instruction manual somewhere. As typical with most designers, the idea came to me one day while I was doing something else. Having my notepad handy, I jotted down this one particular design pattern I saw, and upon returning home tested it out to see if it would work in my hallway. Fortunately for me it did, and the design pattern that I happened to come across that one day was the one that solved my hallway problem! Happily I was able to continue on with my flooring project.

"The Solution"

My solution was to lay the flooring the entire length of the longest wall *First*. Then at the end of the wall extend a *perpendicular line* outward going toward the opposite wall. This new line formed the edge of the floor pattern. However, this outer edge boundary did not extend the full width of the hallway, but instead ended about six inches short of the opposite wall. At this end point, I then made a *sharp angled line* extending all the way until it connected to the shorter length wall. When completed this sharp angle now tied both sides together making the hallway area its own separate identity space.

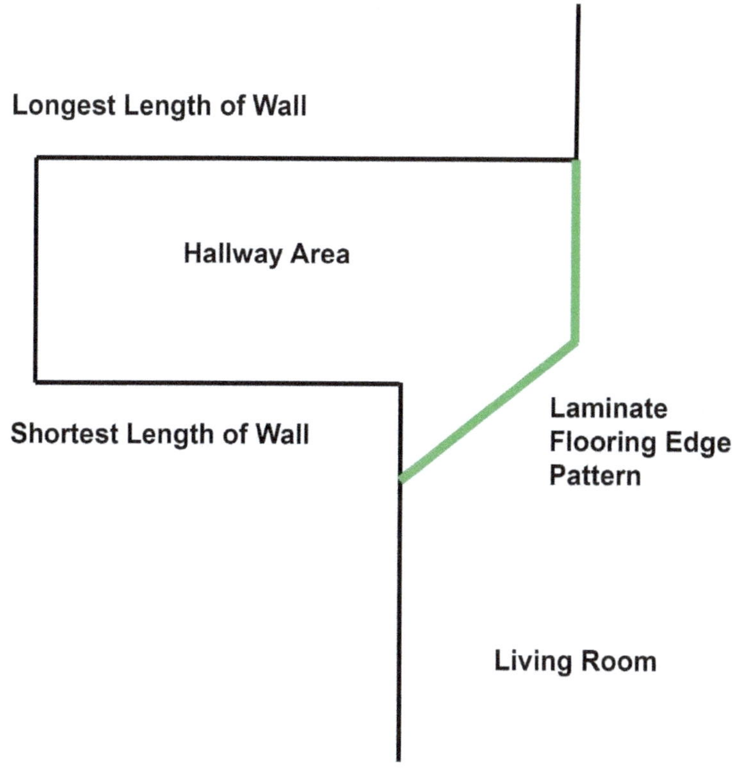

one*Last*Note

Artwork, flooring, decorative molding and trim, or accent colors, which one will it be? Go ahead, choose your weapon! Pick up some paint, lay down some flooring or hang a painting in your entryway. People will notice! Whichever one you choose, you can be assured your home will thank you, and it will never look the same again!

www.ingramcontent.com/pod-product-compliance
Lightning Source LLC
Chambersburg PA
CBHW050958050726

47592CB00007B/2627